RAJPUT – IN SEARCH OF IDENTITY!
Challenges to Religious Syncretism

Asif Iqbal

AAKAR

In Association with

ŚRUTI

Society for Rural Urban & Tribal Initiative

Rajput–in search of identity!
by Asif Iqbal

First Published, 2009

ISBN 978-81-89833-88-6

Published by
AAKAR BOOKS
28 E Pocket IV, Mayur Vihar Phase I, Delhi-110 091
Phone : 011-2279 5505 Telefax : 011-2279 5641
aakarbooks@gmail.com; www.aakarbooks.com

In association with
SRUTI
Q-1, Hauz Khas Enclave, New Delhi-110 016
Web : www.sruti.org.in
E-mail : sruti@vsnl.com

Printed at
Arpit Printographers, Delhi-110 032
E-mail : arpitprinto@yahoo.com
Ph. : 9350809192

Preface

Religion and caste have always been influential in deciding the fate of rulers and their power, in monarchies as well as in democracies. Throughout history we find that religious and political institutions have challenged each other and competed for power. But, gradually they developed a tacit understanding that allowed a symbiotic relationship to emerge. The existence of *raj purohits* and *ulemas* is a good example of how religion works in tandem with the state in kingdoms. This relationship of mutual dependence continues even today. In retrospect, we find this relationship to be harmful for the masses and this was considered an aspect of importance even when the Constitution of India was being drafted; an attempt to separate the modern state from religion was made in our constitution. Enshrined in our Preamble is the proud fact that India is a "secular" country. To reform the inconsiderate attitude that the state had towards the marginalized sections of society the 'welfare role of religion' was transferred to the state itself, following a prolonged debate between the erstwhile political intelligentsia. Unfortunately, the dream of a "just society" that the modern state carried was not realized and this in turn led to the return of religious insecurities.

The concerned civil society and the polity have been struggling hard (since India became Republic in 1950) to strengthen the secular and democratic nature of the Indian state. However, there is an obvious disparity between the practice and the preaching of political parties, as they are concerned only with preserving their vote banks. They know the sinister consequences of sustaining deep-rooted religious and caste based beliefs in society and yet they consciously make use of these "social tools" as their gateway to power; all major political parties use the religious card. While some do it openly, others do it in a less obvious manner. These parties promote religious insecurities both in majority and minority communities and in their activities they complement each other. The demolition of the Babri Masjid, killing of Sikhs in the year 1984 and the Gujarat riots are glaring examples of thriving communal politics.

Taking into consideration the growing polarization in major religious communities in Rajasthan, we at SRUTI felt an urgent need to understand and document these incidences and I decided to start my documentation from a community that has been practicing syncretism (mixed religious practices) for the last six or seven hundred years. The Cheeta-Mehrat-Kathat community which is the subject of study in this report has been witnessing religious politics in the name of 'a historical folly'. I have written this report on the basis of prevalent anecdotes in the community and have made an attempt to explore the available documentary facts with the help of stories from the community that I gathered during my visits to the region.

Generally communalism manifests itself in the form of riots or open conflict between people of separate faiths. This report is an effort to capture the prevailing religious politics within the people of a common faith. It seeks to explore the manner in which the current situation can lead to a possible conflict in the future. Through this report I have tried to highlight factors that are generally considered petty and unimportant but are crucial in the development of fanaticism.

I sincerely hope that this document will prove helpful in understanding the role of different religious groups in a syncretistic community of India, a role which is more or less common to most other suppressed communities in our country. The report should be helpful to the activists who are working at grass-roots level in India.

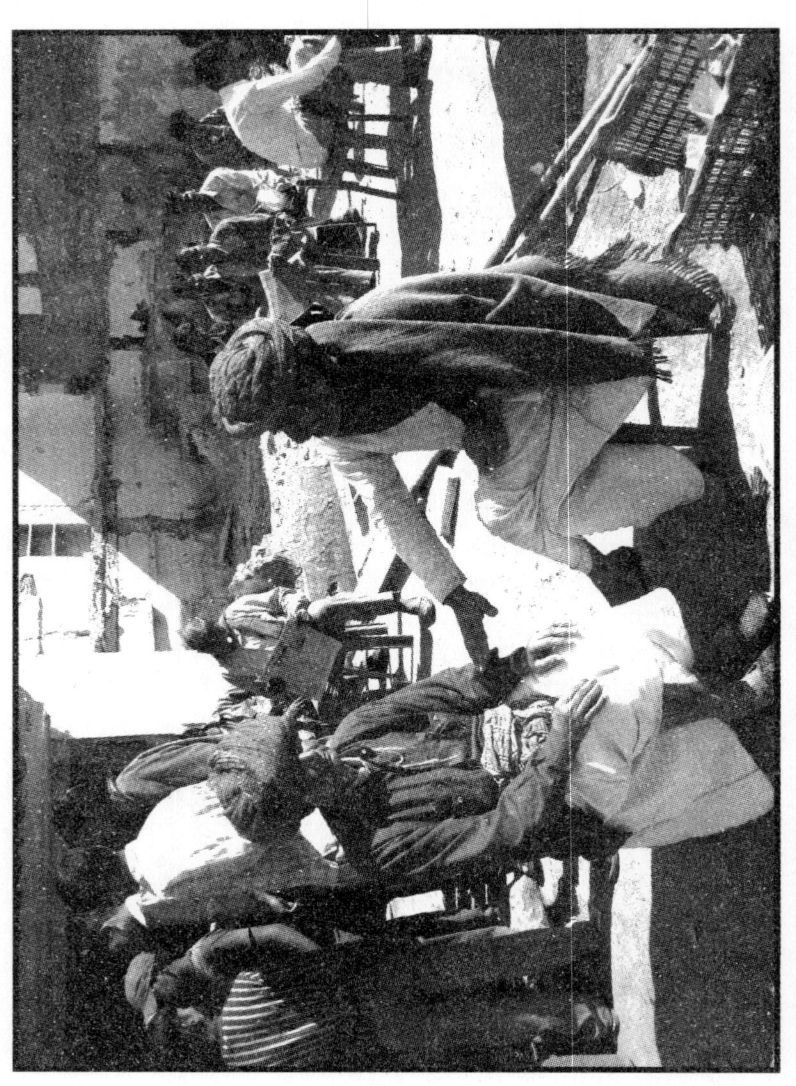

Acknowledgements

I must first acknowledge the debt I owe to Karuna, from whom I came to know of the Cheeta-Mehrat-Kathat-Ghodat community during my visit to Ajmer in 2006. I managed to make a short visit to the nearest village of the community and was able to meet a few people who confirmed their religious syncretism. I decided to come back and spend a few days in the village to learn more about them but couldn't do that till last year when I chose to write a status report on communal politics in Rajasthan. The decision of writing the status report was taken on the basis of regular feedbacks from SRUTI Fellows (based in Rajasthan) about growing communal hatred in their work areas. Initially we at SRUTI decided to hire a jeep for fifteen or twenty days and travel to different regions of Rajasthan which were witness to communal politics. I began with a short visit to this community with Yogi Sikand who has vast knowledge about the syncretistic communities in India. Yogi Sikand has written extensively about the history and faith of Meos. Like the Cheeta-Mehrat, the Meos too have had a history of syncretism. During my first visit I realized that I would need more time to understand and document my findings about the community, considering the vastness of the region they inhabit. I especially want to thank Chand Bhai Cheeta who spent time with me during each visit. My detailed discussions with him helped me in understanding the community. It was because of his help that I could easily reach various other leaders in the community.

I would also like to thank Prof. Jalaluddin Kathat, Peeru Kathat, Shafi Mohammad and other such respected individuals who are dedicated to the task of improving the socio-political scenario of this community and are given heart and soul to their roles as the leaders of Cheeta-Mehrat (Kathat) Mahasabha. They shared with me valuable experiences of political and religious discrimination against their community, often with reference to documents in possession of the Mahasabha. Gulab Singh took out time from his busy schedule to speak to me about his experience of working with the community and I really appreciate his willingness to share with me information concerning the endeavors of the Rajasthan Cheeta Mehrat Magra Merwada Mahasabha. Many other important individuals like Mangi Lal Kathat, Bhawar Singh Chouhan, Rama Kathat, Mumtaz Ali Saheb, Mohammad Baksha Qureshi Saheb, Mohabbat Khan and all others whose names are not mentioned here, helped me by providing precious information.

I got the opportunity of meeting Noora Kathat, ex-MLA (CPI) at his new house at Balesia Nandwada. In fact in his enthusiasm and magnanimity he even arranged for my conveyance to his house from the city. The information that he was able to provide on the rise and fall of the influence of communist ideologies in the community was very interesting indeed. Conversations with Atma Ram, a Jaga and Abdul Gaffar Shah, a Sai (fakir) proved very helpful in clarifying and building upon the findings that my efforts yielded. Ram Singh Rawat got me acquainted with Panna Singh Rawat, an octogenarian who gave me some very valuable historical facts concerning the Rawat community.

Dr. Vasudev Mangal in a remarkable show of kindness gave me a lot of his time and shared with me information and literature of the area that has helped in putting into perspective the currents state of the community. Mohammad Iqbal, a correspondent for 'The Hindu' showed me various paper clippings that proved helpful in analyzing the growth of communalism in Rajasthan. It was Rohitji who had stirred me into taking up this study. His guidance was vital in documentation and finalization of this report. His inputs have helped me in developing a political understanding that allowed for a reasonable critical interpretation of the data this situation provided.

I am grateful to Ranu who used to hear me out very patiently and helped me in evaluating my findings through daily discussions which took place at home or during my visits. Her extraordinary ability to interpret seemingly very intricate issues with the help of parallels with simple examples from daily life cleared my head very often. Without her support and encouragement this study would have been quite impossible.

Altar in a Cheeta house

Mazaar in a village

Rajput – in search of identity!

"Inmey bigaad aa gaya hai" (they have been tainted with the passage of time) or *"inmey ilm ki kami hai"* (they lack wisdom) are the general statements that are used by people to describe the syncretistic nature of the Cheeta-Mehrat-Kathat-Ghodat community, that lives in the vicinity of Ajmer and Beawer in Rajasthan. Surprisingly, one can hear such statements from the current leaders of the community as well. "My name is Ranjeet Singh" says a Cheeta boy and giggles fill the air. "I am Muslim" claims Ranjeet Singh, and the giggles turn into laughter. It is strange that a Pathan family living in the village Ajaiser (barely ten kilometers from Ajmer), more than ninety per cent of whose population is of the Cheeta community is unable to understand Ranjeet and makes fun of him. The same is the fate of many others of the community.

Salim Khan keeps pictures of Hindu deities and local Rajasthani folk heroes in an altar in his hut, and is also regular in his visits to a neighboring *dargah* of a Muslim saint. He says he is a Muslim, but like many in his village he does not know the *Kalima Shahadat*, the Muslim creed of faith. His neighbour (who is also a first cousin) Madho Singh has been offering Eid prayers in the village Eidgah for as long as he can remember. Yet like everybody in his village, he also celebrates Holi and Diwali with gusto. These fascinating people who defy conventional notions of 'Hindu' or 'Muslim' belong to the little-known community called Cheeta – Mehrat - Kathat. Spread across a hundred and sixty villages this community has a population of over five lakhs.

Though the visit I made to this area to satisfy my curiosity was short, I got many more opportunities during last year and it were these visits that helped me in understanding the community and its views on Islam as well as Hinduism better. In this report whose idea as I have mentioned grew directly from my initial curiosity, I have tried to elucidate the historical background of the community so that readers are able to understand the reasons responsible for the spread of faith based prejudices; it should also help in reflecting over past views of the community on matters concerning faith.

Origin of the Mair

The Cheeta-Mehrat-Kathats are also called the Mair or Mer. 'Mair' was first used by the British to refer to the inhabitants of Mairwara. According to beliefs held by the Cheeta-Mehrat, the original Mair were tribes that inhabited the region before them. These tribes were chased out by the Cheeta-Mehrat community and though they moved to the southern parts of Rajasthan, they left their name behind and it was taken by the new inhabitants. I will continue to use the term 'Mair' to refer to the Cheeta-Mehrat.

The Mair became a major threat to traders and other to pilgrims who visited Pushkar and Ajmer. They gained a reputation of being robbers and their villages never paid taxes to the princely states. They would ambush passing traders using the help they got from the cover of surrounding hills. Call it notoriety or call it fame, truth be told they managed to attract all kinds of outcasts from surrounding regions, people who had been ostracized by their own communities. These were not only lower caste people; they also included some people of the higher castes. Col. Dixon writes about two Rajput brothers belonging to the Gehlot caste, who fleeing from Allouddin Ghoree, then the Emperor of Delhi, came for refuge here in 1303 A.D.

There are only a few sources of information regarding the origin of the Mair. First come the accounts of the elders of the community and the writings of the British during their rule in India. Then there are records of families kept by the Jagas, also known as Bahi-Bhat. The script in which these records are written resemble Devnagri but one can rely only on the Jagas for decoding the texts written by them or their ancestors. Both sources claim that the Cheeta-Mehrat-Kathat-Ghodat community is connected to Prithvi Raj Chouhan (1168 – 1192). Prithvi Raj Chouhan's son or Nephew Jodh Lakhan fathered two sons by a woman called Sehdeo who was an Asawaree Meena by caste. His sons were called Anhail and Anoop (also known as Anab). Due to their "mixed parentage" they could not enjoy royal status and were forced to migrate to a village far from Ajmer. What Jodh Lakhan did after the knowledge of Sehdeo's caste spread remains unclear. He either moved out with his family or continued to stay in the fort. In any case it does not make a difference, as the mother and her two sons faced social ostracisation and were forced to take refuge in the hinterlands. With time the community that the sons seemed to have formed in Mairwara, grew in number as well as power. Col. Dixon in his "Sketch of Mairwara", wrote:

> **'...Mairwara forms a portion of the Arabala chain of hills, running from Goozerat to within a few miles of Delhi. It is bounded by Ajmeer to the north, and separates Meywar on the east from Marwar on the west; to the south are the hill possessions of Maywar. It extends over about one hundred miles in length, the line of hills running north-east and south-west. The breath is variable, being chiefly regulated by the width or narrowness of the range. Thus the northern portion has a span of form twenty-five to thirty miles, while to the south to the south the width is restricted to a few miles.'**

Evolution of different clans of Mair

Cheeta and Barad

The generations coming after Anhail and Anoop, already known for their "impure blood" became even more infamous in surrounding areas because of their criminal exploits. This became a problem for girls seeking marriage in other communities. Hindu communities were opposed to intra-caste alliances so the situation of the Mair became worse. As a result for many years female infanticide became an accepted practice. Marriage for the men of the community was never a problem as they would abduct women, or would pressurize people from other more timid communities to give them their girls in marriage. However as time passed either because other communities began to fight back, or because of some form of 'self-enlightenment' the Mair put an end to such practices and made an important decision that led to the origin of the Cheeta and Barads from among the Mair.

A massive meeting was called, in which the Mair leaders from different villages came. Nobody knows the exact date of this historical meeting, but they know that the meeting was held in the temple of their deity. The people believe that a branch of an old tree, under which the participants in the meeting were seated, broke with a noise. It made a loud noise that sounded like "Charad" and the descendents of Anhail who were sitting near that particular portion of the tree were named Charnata or "Cheeta". The descendants of Anoop were called "Barnata" (antonym of Charad in local language) or Barad and hence two clans (gotras) were created from among the Mair. The problem of marriage was solved for nuptial alliances could be formed between persons of different clans. Although, it was decided in the meeting that killing of girls would not be allowed anymore, their reputation as dacoits stayed with the community. Both clans continued with their old ways of looting and settled around Nousar Ghati (valley), and later divided into twenty-four sub clans.

Mehrat

All the clans involved in the 'profession' of looting developed a sort of affinity and would extend support when any of them were in need. According to popular belief, a man from the Barnata clan, Biram one night took shelter in a house belonging to person from his clan. Unfortunately, it so happened that there were no men in the house that night. The woman of the house, Haiwai Pokharni was turned out by her husband who questioned her chastity. Haiwai went to Biram's house and told him of her woe. Biram thinking himself responsible for her condition offered her shelter and asked her to stay with him. The woman bore Biram a son called Dooda. On the day of the 'umbilical cord burial ceremony', the parents found a bag full of Moharen (golden coins) and an additional title, 'Mehrat' attached itself to the baby. The baby led to the birth of a new clan called Mehrat.

Kathat and Ghodat

The Kathat and the Ghodat clans originated together. Two brothers, Harraj and Gajraj from the Mehrat clan joined the army of an Emperor. One night, when the two were on duty, a massive hail storm hit the area and it was followed by heavy rains. While all others ran for cover they did not abandon their duty. While Harraj braved the downpour covering himself with his shield, Gajraj simply kept his seat on his horse all night till the switchover of duty was scheduled. On learning of their dedication the Emperor honored Harraj and Gajraj with the names of Kathat (meaning strong) and Ghodat (referring to horse) respectively. This led to the origin of the Kathat and Ghodat clans.

Origin of Syncretism – Some Prevalent Beliefs

There are different stories and anecdotes related to the origin of syncretistic (mixed religious) practices in the Mair. The community is known to follow three well known practices of Islam. These are *khatna* (circumcision) in males, *halal* (a way of slaughtering animal among Muslims) and *dafn* (burial after death). The following are the prevalent beliefs behind the practice of these Islamic traditions.

1. Influence of a new faith

Sufism is known for its magnanimity and open-mindedness. It does not dispute the manner of praying and other such aspects of religious practice. Economic background is not a consideration among its followers. It is believed that the Mair, facing ostracisation everywhere found acceptance and solace in Sufism. This belief is especially prevalent in the Muslim fraternity associated with Sufism in Ajmer. They believe that Harraj voluntarily accepted Islam under the influence of Sufism propagated by Hazrat Khwaja Moinuddin Chishti in the region. It is said that Harraj is also known as Pir Har Raj, having received the honorific title of Pir, which is used for Muslim saints.

2. Forced conversion

A Mair called Selar was chief of the state of Badnour that was annexed by Rana Kumbha (1433 – 1468). In an attempt to regain his control on Badnour, Selar sought help from Nourang, the king of Agra. The condition that the king of Agra laid down in return for lending Selar his army was that the latter convert to Islam. Selar, desperate to retain his lost pride accepted the three essentials for conversion. He went through circumcision and ate *halal* meat to prove his acceptance of Islam. But on learning that the king had announced publicly the news of his conversion he was infuriated and he left Agra without the king's army.

His attempt to regain control on Badnour failed and he and his companions committed suicide. However Harraj and other followers of Selar started practicing the three essential traditions to be a Muslim.

However according to tales there is another reason behind conversions. An unknown, invading Muslim Sultan evidently gave Harraj, the choice of converting to Islam or dying and having his women folk raped. Harraj chose conversion but instead of fully converting to Islam, he accepted just the three necessary customs. This explains why, most Cheeta-Mehrat still follow these three Islamic practices, while being almost indistinguishable from other local Hindu communities in other respects.

3. Conversion for Security

A somewhat different version of the same story relates that Muslim Sultan gave Harraj a sizeable estate as a reward for giving up his community's practice of raiding trading caravans. This made Harraj's six brothers jealous, and because of them Harraj chose to become a Muslim, feeling that a Muslim Sultan had treated him better than his own kin. However, despite his conversion to Islam, his descendents, the Cheeta-Mehrat, retained only a small link with Islam.

The idea of forced conversion does not explain why this community still persists in practicing Muslim customs. Usually forceful imposition persists only as long as the force exists and does not continue after the threat diminishes. It is possible that the idea of forceful conversion is been propagated by Hindu extremists. Conversion due to security reasons or due to the appeal of a new generous faith seems a more likely reason. To my mind, social recognition was the primary concern for Mair once they grew in power. Outcastes as they were, mistreated by most other communities, a slight encouragement from the Muslim rulers might have been reason enough for the community to adopt Islam. While the Ghodat stopped the three Islamic practices after three generations, the Cheeta and the Mehrat-Kathat continued with them.

Mair during British Period

The Mair were a tough community to control, we learn from the accounts of Col. C.J. Dixon ("Sketch of Mairwara") written in 1858. Following is a list of unsuccessful attempts made by various powers to tame the mighty Mair:

1754 – Rana of Udaipur attacked Mair fort of Huttoon
1778 – Bijee Singh, King of Jodhpur attacked Chang
1778 – Arjun Singh, Thakur of Raipur attacked Kot – Kuranah
1790 – Thakur of Kunthaleah attacked Bhaelan
1800 - 1802 – Sewahjee Nana, Soobedar of Ajmer attacked villages of Jak and Shamgarh
1807 – Baleh Rao attacked Mair
1810 – Mohd. Shah Khan and Rajah Bahadur of Tonk attacked Jak
1816 – Bhim Singh, Rana of Udipur attacked Burar

There were two main reasons why the Mair were targeted repeatedly. First was that they never gave the *lagaan* or *ismaran* (tax) to any princely states and second, as mentioned earlier they were a constant threat to traders and their families living at the periphery of the fort. In fact, they sometimes went so far as to levy the villages for sparing them from their plundering ways. The success with which they managed their admittedly sinister affairs depended upon their unity and not on any leadership. They never selected leaders but had affiliations with four Dangs (villages) namely Jodhaji, Karnaji, Cheetaji and Mehraji. They overwhelmed attackers with their unity and combat skills, which they had mastered because of continued existence in the rough terrains of Aravali Hills. One can still see the remains of few Thanas (police posts) made by the British to protect traders but these could never really control the Mair.

Captain Hall, Major Lawry, and Captain Todd on different occasions tried to bring the Mair under control but remained unsuccessful. Later Lieutenant-Colonel W.G. Maxwell attacked and conquered the Hattoon fort and other important power centers from which the Mair operated. Mairwara was under the control of Merwar, Marwar and the British after it was conquered by the British forces in early 19th century. The villages were divided according to their loyalties or in consideration with strategic locations that the British needed to control the surrounding princely States. The region was divided into nine *parganah* (sectors) out of which, four including Beawer remained under British governance. The British realized the importance of taming the Mair who resided in villages around the city, for they knew that it could help them in gaining greater influence in the area. So they selected Beawer to house their army and gradually it took shape of a cantonment.

Mairwara preserved its reputation of being an ideal destination for outlaws and outcastes even during the British period. Beawer had been a vital political ground for many political leaders during and after the Independence struggle. Shyamgadh fort had been a center of activity for renowned political leaders like Nanaji Fadanvis, Tantya Topey, Ras Bihari Bose, Chandra Shekhar Azad, Sardar Bhagat Singh, Mammathnath Gupt, Kesri Singh Barhat, Pratap Singh Barhat, Jorawar Singh Barhat, Thakur Gopal Singh Kharwa, Vijay Singh Pathik, Arjunlal Sethi, Seth Damodardas Rathi, Seth Gheesuram Jajodia, Swami Kumaranand, Shyamji Krishna Verma etc. It has also been an important place for political development of persons like Mohanlal Sukhadia, Jai Narayan Vyas and Bhairon Singh Shekhawat.

Efforts of Col. Dixon

The foundation stone of Beawer was laid by Lieutenant Colonel C.J. Dixon in early 19th century near the existing

Ajmeri Gate. Col. Dixon was commander of 144 Merwada Regiment and it was under him that the city developed into a cantonment, the main reason being to protect traders during their journeys from notorious Mair leaders like Athoon and Chang Khan and to offer them a safe place for trade. The best way of controlling the Mair was to assimilate them into the daily life activities like those of other communities and hence regular attempts were made to get them involved in farming or the army. The British would recruit youths from among the Mair, considering their marshal background an asset. Col. Dixon took several initiatives to assimilate into the mainstream the notorious local clans that resided in the vicinity. The colonel married a local woman and was the person responsible for the setting up of two important fairs namely the *Teja Mela* and *Dhulandi Mela*. The Colonel's grave lies in a cemetery near a railway crossing and that of his wife, Begam Sahiba lies opposite to the Ramdwara near the Ajmeri Gate at Beawer.

Economy of the Region

Economic documentation of Beawer was essential in the report because it has been an important hub of activities since the British & the town has concentration of Mair population in and around it. Beawer was the leading city of Rajasthan in terms of business and trading. In fact it was also known as the Manchester of Rajasthan because of its three cloth manufacturing mills and many cotton ginning mills. There were also some big units that manufactured *bidi* and employed women. The city was the second largest wool trading market after Fazilka (now in Punjab) in all of India and used to supply cloth, cotton, *bidi*, golden threads, *abhrak* (Gypsum), *surma* etc. to other parts of Rajasthan. Cotton was also exported and therefore several foreign private trading companies had set up their offices in the city.

Since then the factories have been shut down and the area has been utilized for the construction of housing colonies but the city still maintains its commercial status. There are more than two hundred manufacturing units around Beawer that are engaged in producing cement mesh, asbestos pipes, stones and tiles, printing and dying apparatus, handlooms, power looms, plastic papers etc and it still has several SMEs (small and medium enterprises). A huge cement production factory called Shree Cement Limited is located barely seven kilometers from the city on the Masooda road. The factory apparently has an annual turnover of 63.39 lakh tons (FY 2007-08) generating a revenue of crores of rupees for the state government. There are various leading banks in the city that offer credit to business enterprises. Beawer is located on the meter gauge railway line of Western Railways that connects Delhi with Ahmedabad. Major cities like Jaipur, Jodhpur and Udaipur lie at almost equal distances from Beawer and are connected to it by the NH – 8.

The present economic setup of the region relies heavily on the population (10-11 lakhs) of the Cheeta-Mehrat-Kathat-Ghodat and the Rawat communities. This population provides labour to the existing SMEs as well as to trading units. These people are also major consumers of commodities. Most expenditure goes into marriage ceremonies, child birth, death ceremonies and festivals. Each family spends over Rs.40000 on food, medicines and festivals each year. More than a lakh is spent at least in a lifetime on marriage, birth and death ceremonies. This is one of the reasons why communal forces have been kept at bay in the city. An attempt at *bandh*, called by the VHP, failed last year because the local Baniyas (trading community) refused to join it.

The majority of the Mair families are poor as the people have very few sources of income. Most of them are small scale farmers who rely on monsoons for the only crop they sow. Members from most families work in nearby cities as daily wagers and over a lakh have migrated to big cities like Delhi and Kota; Delhi alone is home to over fifty thousand from this community. They are under regular debts as they take money from the money lenders for meeting their annual expenses. A few lucky individuals have been able to find jobs in the Indian Army or in West Asia and consequently the condition of their families is better.

Threats to Syncretism

The Mair pray to different deities like Kalka Mata, Nagpal Dev, Nandrai Mata, Ashapuri Devi, Veer Nejaji Maharaj, Ajaipal Jogi, Rama Peer and so on. They also have mosques in their villages. Their prayers are confined merely to bowing or folding hands to show their respect when in front of temples or mosques. They don't know the rituals essential for a Hindu *puja* or for the *namaz,* nor are they interested in learning these rituals. Their affiliations to either religion seem superficial and come out only during festivals like Eid, Holi, Diwali etc when their celebrations extend to up to a week. Most of the older men wear red *pagdis* (head gear) and Dhotis whereas, women wear *ghagra-choli.* They speak Merwadi which is a mixture of the Mewadi and Marwadi dialects.

Religious groups considered this syncretistic community an ideal place to spread their respective faiths. These groups fight among themselves constantly throwing blame on each other for giving money to get converts. The VHP blames Muslims for bringing in petro-dollars from West Asian Islamic countries for Islamization of the Mair. Tablighi Jamaat and other Muslim organizations claim that the propagation of Hinduism is sponsored by money from the NRIs in the US. The Rawat community in turn claims that an inflow of Euros from European countries is used for the promotion of Christianity among the Rawats; conversions to Christianity are allegedly done through the Church and through NGOs. The CNI (Church of North India) and the CSI (Church of South India) are both active in some villages where Rawats are in majority but even then their presence is almost negligible in comparison to the other two key religious groups. Mair leaders close to VHP allege that the Jamaat and the Churches offer monetary incentives to families for wearing beard, cap or cross. Whereas the leaders who favor the complete Islamisation of the Mair allege that VHP gives money to families for wearing typical Hindu symbols and for solemnizing marriages according to Hindu traditions. Majority of the Mair are reluctant to give up their old ways and it is still common to find a man with two names, for instance the same man could be called Rama Kathat as well as Rehmatullah. There are of course others who have completely embraced one religion and have given up one of their two names so as depict their new singular monologic identity.

1. Influence of Hinduism

In the 1920s the Arya Samaj put in concerted efforts to bring inside Hindu folds various communities like the Cheeta-Mehrat. The powerful Rajput Sabha appealed to the Cheeta-Mehrat to abandon their Islamic practices and turn Hindu. Some Cheeta-Mehrat apparently responded to the call and accepted Hinduism fully.

Since then, time and again reports of conversions of Muslim families to Hinduism have appeared in the media. These reports also drew the attention of various leaders from other religious sects towards the Mair and their syncretistic practices. The decade of 1980 to 1990 comprised a crucial period of time which brought various religious groups and associated political parties into the region. Historically being the hub of political activities in this region Beawer understandably became the operating center for religious activities too. The VHP have built a Temple of goddess Asapurni and as well as a school here in 1991. In 2001-02, an organization called the Rajasthan Cheeta Mehrat Magra Merwada Mahasabha was registered by the VHP to 'counter' the activities of an older organization known as the Rajasthan Cheeta – Mehrat (Kathat) Mahasabha which had been dealing with the Mair 'issue' since 1949.

In some parts of Ajmer, particularly in the Mehrat dominated belt around Beawar, the VHP has been able to convert many to Hinduism. Most of these converts belong to the Gola or Dharampoot sub-caste. These people have traditionally worked as servants of the Mehrat and were (mis)treated as 'low castes'. However, in more recent times other Cheeta and Mehrat have also come under the influence of the Parishad, which has set up a number of temples, schools and clinics in the area, so as to attract the poverty-stricken people and spread its 'message'. The Parishad harps upon the 'fact' that the Cheeta-Mehrat are descendents of Prithiviraj Chauhan and alleges that their ancestors were converted to Islam through force. Some people of the community accept conversion to Hinduism because a distinctive Hindu, Rajput identity can help them climb up the social ladder.

The VHP publicly denounces those Mair who visit *mazaars* and those who follow any Muslim customs or practice Islamic rituals for instance ones of *Nikah* (marriage). They try to make Mair syncretism seem a bad practice and then use the effect this maneuver has to push them into converting to Hinduism. *Prasad* (offerings) of Ram Devra was distributed in the community, presumably by the VHP and photographs of the event were published newspapers. Most families seem to take a neutral stand over the VHPs politics of *paravartan* (re-conversion) for they fear that if they denounce it they might incur the wrath of the 'Almighty'. Only those of the community who seem to have understood the VHP's politics and some others who have been drawn closer to other religions are able to distance themselves from this process of conversion to Hinduism.

Various people have varied opinions on the reports of mass conversions of Cheeta-Mehrat to Hinduism through *shuddhi* or 'purification' ceremonies. While the advocates of *hindutva* see these to be victories, some Cheeta-Mehrat who wish to retain their centuries'-old identity dismiss these reports as cheap publicity gimmicks arranged to 'demoralize' the community. There is strong resistance among most sections of the community to the idea of *ghar-vapasi* (conversion to original faith). Those who resist feel that not only would this mean going against the 'promise' of their ancestor Pir Harraj but also that even if they were to become Hindus, the other Hindus would still refuse to establish conjugal ties with them, seeing their Muslim associations as having somehow 'tainted' or 'polluted' them. Hence, most people of the community refuse to budge, citing the promise that their *baderey* (ancestor), Harraj or *Kathat Dada* (grandfather), is said to have made to a 'Muslim Sultan'. To abandon the Islamic customs that their ancestor had adopted, they believed, would be to go against their wishes.

These activities of the Hindu right wing among the Mair have once again made clear their intentions of making India into a Hindu nation. People who condone their actions, construing them as retaliatory and 'provoked' by the activities of other religious groups must rethink their stand. The VHP leadership in Beawer is clearly not ready to accept the syncretism of the Mair. In fact even the last BJP government of the state was keen on passing the Religious Freedom Bill in the state assembly. The bill, once passed, will seal the fate of those Mair who at some point or another call themselves Hindu.

Islamic Influence

Islamic groups active in the region, particularly the Jamiat ul-Ulema-e Hind, the Tablighi Jamaat and the Hyderabad-based Tamir-e Millat, have set up numerous *madarsas* and mosques and this has had a visible impact. Most agree that the last two decades have witnessed a considerable degree of Islamisation in the community despite the opposition of Hindu groups and hostile elements in the government. The community is so much of an attraction for religious sects that the even Ahmadias, (a less known and marginalized faction of Islam) struggling for their existence in India, are also trying their luck with the Mair. Obvious results of religious conversions are loss of caste symbols like turban, dhoti and *ghaghra-choli* of the Mair and the adorning of religious symbols like cap, beard, *tilak*, saffron scarf and longer body covering attires in women.

Ever since the commencement of syncretism in Mair, Islamic groups have been trying to make the Cheeta-Mehrat accept Islam completely. Right at the beginning, mosques were built in each village and one Sai (the Sai are affiliated to the Madar family of Barelvi faction of Islam) family per village was deputed by the Muslim rulers. The Sai or fakirs were easily absorbed in the community because of their flexible approach to syncretistic practices. However, their role as religious preachers, in course of time got reduced to ritualistic slaughtering of animals and burial of the dead. The coming of new Maulvis from the Deobandi faction in the 1980s further reduced the role of the Sai. Furthermore because the Sai depended upon donations in kind (food etc.) from Mair households, the latter could not stand the notion of them being equal and developed a dislike for the Sai.

It wasn't easy for the maulvis to establish themselves. "I was forced to slaughter a goat in front of a deity during a festival. After the slaughter, I was asked to eat the meat too and when I denied, and I was asked to leave the village", a maulvi recollects while giving an account of the time he worked in a Cheeta village. Another maulvi says that, he had to give up saying *fajir azaan* (morning sermons) on a microphone because he was told that it disturbed the surrounding families during their sleep. These were days when the VHP had an active presence in the villages. According to the two maulvis, initially the VHP managed to instigate the Mair against the maulvis but was unable to continue its activities in the Cheeta villages after 1990 because its intentions became clear to the villagers. So even though to begin with the maulvis based in these villages had a tough time their lives are presently trouble free. However their task is still not easy and their work shows slow returns. Very few children come to the *maktabs* in the mosques and the Mair's relationship with the maulvis is largely confined to performing rituals like *niqah, khatna, halal* and *dafn*. They visit the mosques only during the Eids or sometimes for *juma* (Friday *namaaz*). Though a sizable section of Badarkhani (a faction among the Cheeta) families have opened their doors for Islamisation the majority still practices syncretism.

Many Cheeta-Mehrat participate actively in the *ijtimas* (religious discourse) organized by the Jamaat. Their willingness to participate in religious functions of these sorts is part of their traditional beliefs and their participation keeps motivation alive in the activists of Jammat and Tabligh. In reality participation in *ijtimas* is more of a social outing than anything else for the Mair and despite their participation in religious functions organized by different groups they maintain their old syncretistic identity. The rigidities of the caste system have proved helpful in the retention of their syncretistic identity.

Islamisation operates as an alternative vehicle for upward mobility for many Cheeta-Mehrat; in some villages more mosques and *madarasas* have come up and the people have come to identify themselves as 'unambiguously Muslim'. But even in these villages people continue with older habits which are considered unfit for Muslims. For instance alcohol brewing and consumption is still widespread. In addition the people continue to practice the tradition of child-marriages. Some people still have not given up the practice of *nata pratha*, valuation of women, for relationships which are forced. Religious men and community leaders seem to be working hard to curb these practices; as it appears preaching that is religious in nature seems to have greater effect in controlling alcoholism than those that are merely moral. The leaders themselves are too busy struggling to come to terms with a new religious identity, to really be effective in the public realm and in recent times little has been done for the social and economic betterment of the community.

In recent times the Rajasthan Cheeta-Mehrat (Kathat) Mahasabha has been trying to deal with the question of socio-economic growth in the community. The organization, at present, is under control of those leaders from community who in essence seem to be in favour of an 'Islamic purification' of the community. The leadership is planning the removal of the word 'Mehrat' from the name of the Mahasabha because of the greater ambiguity about the religious practices of the Mehrat. Religious fanaticism seems to have grown in Kathat from 1980s onwards and locals blame the VHP for it. The leaders claims VHP's attempts to highlight the idea of *paravartan* in the Cheeta-Mehrat has also brought greater attention from Islamic organizations who have identified the "precarious" nature of the community. The prevalent 'half-Muslim' status of the community has helped in growth of their endeavors towards achievement of making the people of the community 'fully-Muslim'.

Christian Influence

New faiths always attract people in times of socio-economic distress and Mair are no exception. If proselytizers from the two major religions of the country sense bright prospects in the Mair, the Christian proselytizers are not far behind. Finding limited scope in the Cheeta-Mehrat-Kathat-Ghodat community at large they have tried to target the oppressed amongst them. Golas or Dharampoots as mentioned before were least privileged among the Mair. They were people from the lower castes who had a slave like status and became free from their bondage only after India became a republic. Christian influence seems to be increasing among this section of the community.

Women of the Community

"Auraton ka koi dharm nahi hota" (women do not have any religion), "why are you arguing about belief in different faiths?" an old man, Shayer Chacha said trying to pacify two men who had gotten into an altercation during my discussions with them. "Women don't have any faith and they don't argue over such things; you must learn from them". The wise old man had intervened to calm down two Mair who claim to be from different faiths. Women are often the oppressed among the oppressed, and are undoubtedly the worst sufferers in any oppressed community.

In recent times there have been attempts aimed to make Mair women more conscious of religion and customs. Greater restrictions have been imposed upon them; they can no longer go to local *melas* (fairs) and are expected to keep from doing certain activities that they were able to do without hesitating earlier. These impositions started strengthening around the period of the national independence struggle period and so far attempts have been made to rethink them. The Mohammad Ali Memorial Higher Secondary School set up at Beawer in 1932 by the Mohammad Ali Memorial Trust Society has residential facility for boys but not for girls and there have been no thoughts given to the building of new hostels for girls. No women participate in the Mahasabha meetings, not even wives of the leaders. While gender equity is a difficult issue for most people in the world, among the Mair where the males are also struggling for a stable social identity the status of women seems to be of no concern to anybody.

Women have the responsibility of performing traditional rituals of the community. They are, as it were the preservers of the old syncretistic tradition. But families that have moved towards a completely Hindu or a completely Muslim identity stop their women from practicing these rituals. In this way another freedom was taken away from these women.

Marriages in the Mair

Sixty-five year old Naseeb Khan recently arranged for his son Prakash Singh to marry Sita, daughter of Ram Singh and his wife Reshma. Three months ago, Hemant Singh's daughter Devi married Lakshman Singh in a *nikah* ceremony solemnized by a Muslim maulvi. Naseeb Singh's elder son Roshan had a Muslim-style *nikah,* and his younger son Iqbal got married in accordance with Hindu traditions. While this sounds usual in the light of the syncretism of the Mair, one wonders if it actually remains regular practice. Such activities have constantly been questioned by the 'puritans'.

I pick upon the question of marriage within the Mair so as to highlight another crucial idea that has influenced the social dynamics of the community. Marriage at present is possible between individuals from the Cheeta and the Mehrat (also known as Kathat) communities only because of prevalent syncretistic practices among them. Earlier marriage between the Cheeta-Mehrat-Kathat, Hindu communities like the Rawat and Muslim communities like the Pathan, Sayyad, Sheikh and Khadim were common. But while Mair would accept brides from the Rawat community, they married their girls only into Muslim communities. The three popular reasons cited for the end of even this practice are:

1. Casteism of the Mair

The Rawat were ready to accept that the girls that got married among the Mair be buried in Mair fashion on the condition that the Mair let Rawat men marry Mair girls as well. Mair refusal put an end to this practice, altogether somewhere in the earlier part of the 20th century. Seemingly, the Mair had some sort of consciousness of being superior in terms of caste to the Rawat and hence would not allow their women to marry Rawat men.

2. Insult of the Rawat

According to a popular tale a girl from a Rawat family was married to a Mair man who was a cobbler by profession. The parents of the girl noticed her assisting her husband in his business in a market. Since cobblers are 'untouchables' in the *Varna* System the Rawat family thought this an affront to their superior social status and rued the fact that they gave their girl to the wrong man. This incident has led to the end of any more marital alliances among families from the two communities. Nobody from either community is able to give any specific information about this matter and one wonders if the story is not another tale instigated by religious groups to brand a particular community.

3. Meeting before the Independence

A huge meeting was organized in Pali district of Sendhda in the year 1947 by Major (Retd.) Fateh Singh Rawat in which around 1 lakh Mair participated. Raja Gaj Singh of Jodhpur presided over the meeting. The meeting was called to express loyalty to India by 'eating of *jhatka* (a process of animal slaughter) meat by the participants. The offer was refused by the Mair as it was against their beliefs which dictated the eating of *halal* meat. Some say this incident was a reason behind the discord that led to the discontinuation of inter-community marriages.

Nobody knows how the practice of *nikah* came into prominence but *nikah* started dominating *pherey* from 1940s onward. Marriages being solemnized according to Hindu traditions are decreasing in number gradually. The uncertainty that surrounds marriage ceremonies of individuals appears to play a crucial role in constraining a person's efforts of gaining non-syncretistic religious identity. Bhawar Singh Chouhan married his daughter off with a heavy heart. He is the Sarpanch of the Ajisar Panchayat, Ajmer and is a strong supporter of the BJP. He wanted to marry his daughter in a Hindu manner and the wedding cards that he distributed invited people to a *vivah* ceremony but much to his dismay he had to make do with a *nikah*. He was forced to accept this decision made by his family and the elders of the Cheeta community. Though as per tradition the decision to perform a Hindu or a Muslim marriage ceremony lays with the girl's family. However in recent times most families have started favouring *nikah* after a collective decision was made by leaders under the influence of religious extremists.

Caste identities prove overbearing on lives even after change of religion and families that have embraced Hinduism or Islam completely often face a lot of problems in their respective communities. The so called 'puritans' in the society disprove of relations with such families and as a result these families have to return to their older ways to be properly accepted. The Cheeta community has two clans, Cheetakhani and Badarkhani (progeny of Bahadur Khan). The Badarkhani, have been trying to embrace Islam through the performance of prevalent Islamic practices in other Muslim communities or by doing things as per the advice of the Maulvis in their village. They are left with very few choices in marriages and have to look for the Badarkhani families in other villages. Similarly, Kathat families that have adopted Islam have to stay away from the Dangs (Cheetaji, Mehraji, Karnaji and Jodhaji) for marital alliances. Surprisingly, both the Islamised Badarkhani and Kathat have not imbibed the custom of consanguineous marriage from other Muslim communities in India.

Often families refused to have their sons circumcised, hoping to provide them with a more clear 'Hindu' identity. However, Mair families were not ready to give their daughters in marriages to such men as the decision was seen as a caste transgression. So often they were circumcised just before marriage and, despite considering themselves 'Hindus', their marriages were solemnized through *nikah* in a Muslim fashion. In any case, only hands full of economically independent Cheeta-Mehrat-Kathat families have dared to practice only one religion.

Religious politics of various sorts have led to a situation where cultural practices like marriage ceremonies have become marks used for social segregation of communities. People who practice a 'pure' religion are not comfortable in giving their girls in marriage to the families that practice 'two religions'. The Rawat were the first to distance themselves from the Mair and later the Badarkhani and the Kathat also drifted apart from other portions of the Mair population.

Failures of the Modern State

"We say *Ram-Ram* to Hindus and *salaam* to Muslims. We hold a *laddu* in each of our hands", said Salim Khan smiling, when I asked him how his community responds to the contradictory appeals of Hindu and Muslim revivalist groups competing with each other. "Most of us do not know how to perform intricate *Brahminical pujas* or say the Muslim *namaaz*. We just bow our heads before temples, mosques and *dargaahs*", he explained. He talked of how after years of syncretism, his community is now becoming divided into two factions—one Hindu and the other Muslim. "Intermarriages still occur, but the number decreases all the time", he lamented. "However", he stressed, "whether Hindu or Muslim, we all think of ourselves as brothers, descended from the same ancestors."

The modern Indian state has taken no active notice of the syncretism of the Mair. The community was overlooked completely in the National Five Year Plans; there were no special economic packages directed towards livelihood activities in this region. Like in most other poor regions of India the essential welfare services that the state should provide like education and health were ignored and schools and health centers were left to deteriorate. Perhaps an analyst can gloss over the lack of representation of the Mair in the government but it is still difficult to understand and ignore some other things in which they have been neglected.

For instance there is no certainty of finding at least some army jobs. In fact the national leadership snapped away one good source of livelihood for the Mair by dissolving the 44 Merwara regiment of the British army in 1946; several men lost their jobs.

The Mair are a 'marshal race' and so was considered for recruitment in the British army without categorizing them into any specific religion. It seems that this has not helped the Mair cause as far as employment in the Indian Army is concerned now. Even though the national leadership approved the recruitment of Mair youth under the Kayamkhani quota (in the Grenadiers group) in the year 1980 under the former Prime Minister Mrs. Indira Gandhi, the Mair are unfortunate to lose the reservation from 2008. The Kayamkhani are a Muslim community from Rajasthan and one can see how a syncretistic community like Mair became victim to politics based upon religion which takes care only of vote-banks. They even lost their reservation under the Kayamkhani quota due to a letter from the Army recruitment center at Jabalpur dated 2nd Jan 2008. Since then they have been struggling for some sort of reservation in the army. The Defense Ministry somehow constantly manages to overlook this community whose people generally fulfill the physical requirements necessary for recruitment. Biased policy decisions at the centre and state level make sure that the Mair demands are not met and these experiences only prove to be constant lessons on politics based on religion and caste. It is interesting to note how a community that never really considered religion to be an important factor in such matters is being forced into the practice by the state apparatus.

It is not hard to understand that the vulnerability of this community to religious politics is at least partly because of the government's callous attitude and its evasion of issues like health and education in the community. Religious groups are able to spread their influence by building and running schools and hospitals. The only active state apparatus is the local police in the form of Intelligence to check the traces of "anti-national" activities in Mair. Furthermore the manner in which the state has failed to make any provisions for the syncretism that the community practices causes more problems. Though the admission forms to government run primary schools does not ask for the candidate's religion but the birth certificate does and their the child get marked as Muslim because of the practice of circumcision in the mair.

My intentions here are not to question the provisions of religious freedom (under Article 25), that our Constitution provides. However we cannot disregard the unfortunate fact the propagation of particular religions, at least in the here and now is undoubtedly connected with the undermining of other religious interests. It is important in such a situation to repeatedly question and improve the limited role of civil structures. The zeal for social change has undeniably been missing in their endeavors and this has allowed the free growth of right-wing and fanatic forces. In fact I would go as far as to say that the secular civil society of our country has failed even in checking the growth of fanaticism inside the apparatus of the state. In various ways that I have already mentioned and perhaps due to some others that I have been unable to bring into my report, it is this incompetence on part of governmental agencies that has lead to the free flowering of communal and caste based prejudices among communities like the Mair.

Conclusion

I have spoken at times in this report of the uncertainty that surrounds the reason behind the time of commencement of syncretism in the Mair. Most accounts are biased and all are based more on anecdotes and stories than on solid fact—hopefully this report will help readers understand why there is no conclusive documentation of the fact in question. However I have not dealt at length with this question because the point of the report was to explore the reasons responsible for the growth of communalism and for religious polarization in a community that has historically practiced a form of syncretism.

Every time this matter came up during discussions the elders of the community explained the practice of female feticide by citing the superiority of their 'blood'. In effect they never accepted anybody else as equivalent to them as far as caste was concerned. While the people of this community identified themselves as Rajput, other Rajput communities did not accept their daughters in marriage due to the strange stories surrounding the question of the former community's origin. The claims of this community reflect the rigidity of inter-caste dynamics—they forgotten the manner in which they themselves were victims of casteism. But then, while they were able to overcome their economic problems through robbery and other disrespectful means they could never really attain social parity with the people of other communities and in turn they themselves got sucked into the evil hierarchical caste system. Strangely and to my mind unfortunately, they are still proud of being associated with the Chouhans. They still prefer to hang on to their "half-Chouhan" identity rather than giving it up even though the cause of discrimination against them is this in-between status.

Mair opposition to completely conversion to either Hinduism or Islam is also based upon their singular history. The caste-system is deeply entrenched in the state of Rajasthan and the Cheeta-Mehrat are identified by their syncretism. They do not hold on to their practices due any attachment to them or due to pride, but because of the rigidities of the caste system. Families that do adopt any one religion completely are uncomfortable in their old community, presumably because the people refuse to accept them. Forgetting that they themselves have been victims to such discriminatory practices, the Mair themselves are given to the injustices of the caste system. "Doodh sey dahi to ban sakta hai per, dahi sey doodh kabhi nahi ban sakta" (milk can produce curd but, curd cannot be reconverted into milk.)—was the answer we got from a teacher in the matter of re-conversion. This brings out well the rigidity of caste and religious frameworks in the state.

The Mair leaders are visibly proud of the fact that their history till a short time back had witnessed no religious conflicts. Their continued syncretism due to minimal contact with Hindu or Muslim communities is surely an important reason for this. However in recent times those among them who have embraced one of the two religions completely seem to have an advantage because the option of finding employment in other communities is open to them. As a result it seems probable that religious polarization will get accelerated in the community in the coming years and the greater religious strife might occur, despite the optimism that the leaders seem to derive from their history.

Religion and caste based extremism undoubtedly breed in the soil of social insecurity. For instance till 1978, when the three cloth mills of Beawer were running in profit the penetration of religious forces was minimal. A strong trade union of mill workers, affiliated to the CPI which still has an office close to the mills never gave these forces any space. However with the closure of the mill the trade union due to obvious reasons disintegrated. The social security that the identity of being part of a politically organized work force gave the workers has been lost. With the decline of the Left in the area religious fanaticism has grown. Since then a massive Mosque and a minority (Muslim) school have appeared in the exact area that was earlier used by the factory workers for residence.

Religious groups in their bid to claim as much of the Mair population as possible make use of various sorts of rhetoric. A commonplace among these is to put the blame for their current condition on some imagined or at least half-imagined injury that somebody from another religious community inflicted upon them. As this report shows, Mair history is so interspersed with myths and tales that this ploy has ample ground to work upon. The more important aspect of this history, which is the community's unique religious identity—their syncretism—is completely marginalized. At the same time problems that have socio-economic reasons go unresolved because things barely connected are implicated and blamed. Religious fanaticism is a social problem not just because it creates new hurdles, but also because it does not allow other problems to be addresses.

Because of constant attacks on their historical identity by religious groups, Mair syncretism has losing its dynamism. It fails to attract attention partially because its own people are moving out of it and embracing more conventional religious identities. These groups, as I have tried to highlight again and again succeed in their designs because they provide the community services that should have provided by the state administration. These groups promise the people of the community social and economic upliftment—something that they fail to provide completely. Instead by creating small pockets of relatively better of persons they confuse and destroy the entire sense of a collectivity.

In those who consider religion to be a path to salvation its role as a strengthener of moral values has indeed been vital. For a person who has tested all waters and found nothing, it provides relief. For the destitute of our country it may be such a consolation. I am not out to question the role of religion in human life per se, but I am concerned about the projection of religion as the only possible path to emancipation—especially in a country where religions seem to be keeping in place and spreading, in insidious ways the evils of the caste system.

"We are a unique community," says Rohan Singh. "I don't think there is any other community like us in the whole of India." His mother's brother, Buland Khan, nods in agreement. "Our philosophy of life is to live and let live. People must be free to worship God in whatever way they like", he tells me. 'Some Cheeta-Mehrat', he confesses, "feel ashamed about their identity. Others mock them and say that they are confused and muddled-up and are trying to ride two boats at the same time. But I think we are right. Some of us are Muslims and others are Hindus, like me and my nephew here. But still we live together in harmony. We eat together and we intermarry. Religion is a personal issue and does not effect our relations."

The majority among the Mair still stick to their syncretistic identity and resist forces that try to make them give it up. Nevertheless, the danger to this identity that has lasted for so long, from religious fanaticism is genuine. How this started is an irrelevant question, to my mind. It is important for to us to take note of the lesson that this practice could hold for all on the issue of religious intolerance. It is important that the civil society and people's organisation of Rajasthan take cognizance of the active religious politics in this region that seems to be affecting this unique community in ways that are too good. It is imperative that the state responds with haste and tries to encourage a more secular politics.

References

1. Vol. 38, Anthropological Survey of India
2. Sketch of Mairwara, by Col. C.J. Dixon
3. Rawat- Rajpooton ka Itihas, Thakur Premsingh Chouhan
4. Letters of Rajasthan Cheeta – Mehrat (Kathat) Mahasabha
5. Letters of Rajasthan Cheeta – Mehrat Magra Merwada Mahasabha
6. Articles of The Hindu, Dainik Bhaskar, & Rajasthan Patrika

Kathat children in a village

Asapura Mata temple and school in Beawer